Father to Son

Father to Son

Life Lessons on Raising a Boy

Harry H. Harrison Jr.

WORKMAN PUBLISHING COMPANY • NEW YORK

Library of Congress Cataloging-in-Publication Data

Harrison, Harry H.
  Father to son : life lessons on raising a boy / by Harry H. Harrison Jr.
     p. cm.
  Rev. ed.
  ISBN 978-0-7611-7488-2 (alk. paper)
  1. Fathers and sons. 2. Parenting. 3. Fatherhood. I. Title.
  HQ755.85.H3743 2013
  306.874'2--dc23

                              2012033124

Design by Janet Vicario
Illustrations by Matt Wawiorka

Workman books are available at special discounts when purchased in bulk
for premiums and sales promotions as well as for fund-raising or educational
use. Special editions or book excerpts can also be created to specification.
For details, contact the Special Sales Director at the address below or send
an email to specialmarkets@workman.com.

Workman Publishing Company, Inc.
225 Varick Street
New York, NY 10014-4381
workman.com
fearlessparenting.com

WORKMAN is a registered trademark of Workman Publishing Co., Inc.

Printed in the U.S.A.
First printing March 2013
10 9 8 7 6 5 4 3 2 1

Dedication

Sage and Field taught me everything I know.

Melissa made it all possible.

The Five Keys

Turning a boy into a man is a man's job. Since the beginning of time, it's been up to a father to make his son responsible. Kind. Courageous. Honorable. A young boy doesn't come with instructions. He just comes with boundless love and an adventurous spirit. But the journey to manhood begins very early . . . the first time he looks at his dad and thinks, "I want to be like him."

1.
Be around.

2.

Be his father, not his friend. If you don't understand the difference, imagine his confusion when you must discipline him.

3.
Be a good husband. Show his mom respect at all times.

4.

Be home for dinner.

5.
Be his hero.

Little Boys

Treasure your time
with your son.

Teach him to keep a secret.

Show him how to eat an Oreo. This is a skill that will serve him for his entire life.

Set strict bedtimes
for him as he grows up.
Boys need their sleep.

Makes sure he knows his full name, address, and his parents' names and phone numbers. Many four-year-olds only know their father's name is "Daddy."

Take him for
walks and
introduce him to
the world of bugs.

Read to him
nightly.
He'll love it.

Don't let him sleep in your bed, even if he's scared or sick. Sleep on the floor in his room.

Make an effort to give up drinking and smoking. If he never sees his dad doing those things, they will hold less mystery for him.

Teach him how to
plant a flower.
It involves three things
boys love—
dirt, digging, and
garden hoses.

Teach him to ride
a two-wheel bike.
It means freedom.
Jog alongside.

Accept the fact that he just might play with dolls. It's no big deal.

Ask him what he
did today. Listen.

Show him how to clean his room. Little boys don't just absorb this through osmosis.

Encourage the joy
of learning.

Teach him how to
dial 911 and when
and why.

Buy him something to hang from—a jungle gym or climbing bars. Something.

Show him how
to throw a punch.
Then raise him to
never start a fight.
And teach him to walk
away from one.

Take him on hikes and
show him how to ford
a stream. Let him get
wet and dirty.

Display his
artwork in
your office.
Even that weird
ashtray thing.

Let him hang out with you. Remember, he has a need to be around you, to learn what being a man is all about.

An unhappy boy
is often one who is
hungry or tired.
Or both.

Turn off the TV, turn off the lights, give him a flashlight, and make up stories at night. He won't be able to get enough.

Meet him for
lunch at his school.
Talk to him about
what he's learned.

Talk to him about drugs and alcohol early, from the time he's about five years old. Because if you don't, somebody else will.

Eat breakfast with him. This is how he learns about getting up and going to work.

Take him to a theme park. Ride the rides his mom wouldn't dream of getting on. (At some point, of course, neither will you. Strike while the heart is healthy.)

If you buy him
Superman pajamas,
count on him
launching himself off
counters, chairs,
bunk beds—and
sometimes onto you.

Make sure he learns your cell phone number. Then take his calls. Forever. Even if you're at work.

Teach him magic.

Teach him not
to litter.

Remind him often
to put the seat up.
Then to put the seat
down. Then to flush.

Teach him to
throw up in the toilet,
not on your bed.
Many boys will stagger
past two bathrooms
only to destroy your
bedroom.

Teach him to return what he borrows.

Let him learn the joys of chocolate chip cookie dough.

Reassure him he won't die if he bleeds a little.

Take your son to work with you every now and then. Pay as much attention to him as you do to other people in the office.

Tell him that
sometimes you're
wrong.

Race him.
You'll never forget
the day he
beats you.

Give him responsibility.

Don't let the TV be a babysitter.

Make sure he
knows he's always
safe at home.

Buy him a pet only when he's ready to take care of it. It will teach him to care about something other than himself.

Praise him often.

Teach him to
compliment others.

Don't tolerate temper
tantrums. Not now.
Not when he's fifteen.
Because the world
won't.

Scream at him and
you will raise
a screamer.

Teach him not to hurt others.

Don't let him quit out of frustration. He won't learn anything.

His favorite game for a long, long time will be playing with you. Be available. Even when you're tired. Even when the presentation went south. Be available.

Encourage him to
go barefoot.

Remember that with today's technology, you can still tell him good-night, face-to-face, even if you're on the other side of the world.

Teach him to lock his bike.

Teach him not to be afraid of animals, but to respect them.

Ask him who
his heroes are.
These are the people
he'll copy.

Talk to him about what he wants to be when he grows up. Don't be alarmed by his answer.

Teach him the wonder of gazing at the moon.

Teach him that every life is precious.

Help him to
understand that his
word is his bond.
And remember,
he'll learn from you.

Teach him that if
he waters grass,
it will grow.

It's a fact of life: Some kids—especially boys—have learning disabilities. If he can't read by the time he's five, have him checked out by a doctor.

Buy him a guinea pig or hamster for his first pet, but don't be surprised when he announces he doesn't know where it is.

Remember,
little boys love
their grandfathers.
No one really
knows why.

Without scaring him, talk to him about bad people and what he should do if they approach.

Insist he play outside a lot. It's much healthier than watching TV or spending all day in front of the computer.

Show him how to
pop a wheelie.

Never forget that it's impossible to hug or cuddle or kiss a young boy too much.

Remember,
boys are like lion cubs:
They show their
affection by hugging,
wrestling, and rolling
around on top of
each other.

Don't fight his fights.

Never tell him boys
don't cry. Ask him why
he's crying.

Teach him to clean up his own messes. A lot of eighteen-year-olds still have their moms cleaning up after them.

Allow him to believe in Santa Claus. And the Easter Bunny. And the Tooth Fairy. Promote the sense of wonder. He'll never stop looking for it.

Leave the office early to play with him.

Teach him to share
with his little brother.
(This may take
a few years.
Well, a lot of years.)

Give him
piano lessons,
but realize he may
want to switch to
guitar one day.
Or drums.

Realize there are some things you can't teach him.

Let him watch you shave. This is when he begins to put two and two together.

Teach him to
respect authority,
but not to be in
awe of it.

Encourage him to
make friends with
the white boy,
the black boy,
and the Chinese kid
who doesn't speak
a word of English.

If you spend time
with him and his
friends when
he's young, he won't
think twice about you
being around them
when he's older.

Teach him the joys of peanut butter and honey.

Show him how to
tie a tie and how
to polish his shoes.

Remember—
the values you teach
him now are those
he'll hold as
a teenager.

Check his homework
nightly. Don't leave
this totally up to
his mom. He'll see how
important his studying
is to you.

Even if you can,
don't buy him
everything.

Remember, bullying him is a guaranteed way to raise a bully.

Teach him how to find his way home.

Don't criticize
his mistakes.
Criticize his lack
of effort.

Teach him to spit.
He'll practice it
all day.

Take him
for doughnuts on
Saturday morning.
Let his mom sleep late.

Realize that by the time he's ten, he'll be more adept on the computer than you are. And you won't know how it happened.

Share a big
plate of ribs.
The messier the
better.

Teach him never to be afraid to try new things.

Boys & Sports

Don't forget that when you're a kid, the point of sports is to have fun.

Realize that while he's young, one of your son's favorite things about organized sports will be the uniform. Let him wear it to school.

Try not to miss
his games. A boy loves
playing in front
of his dad and
hearing him cheer.
He'll always ask,
"Did you see me?"

Celebrate after every game.

Show him how to put a baseball in a new glove and wrap a belt around it.

Teach him how to throw a curveball.

Take him fishing.
If he actually
catches something,
it will be the thrill of
his young life.

Take him to the
golf course and
teach him to play.
Even if he's three.
Be patient.

Remember that little boys get distracted by bugs and dirt and lots of other stuff even while a game is happening all around them. Yelling will not change this.

If you find yourself yelling at him or the referee, take a book to the games and go sit far away from everyone else. They'll think you're a bit odd, but your son will appreciate it.

If his coach
is a screamer,
find another team.
If you're the coach,
retire.

Teach him how to swim. If you don't know how, send him for lessons.

Show him how to lift weights.

Take him to hockey games. Boys love the fights (totally politically incorrect, but a fact).

Make him carry his own athletic bag.

Take him
horseback riding.
(It might be
a fifteen-year-old,
three-legged mare,
but he'll remember
a white stallion.)

Do not criticize him
after his games.
He knows exactly
what he did. His coach
will criticize him.
He needs a father to
support him.

Practice with him and he will get better. This goes for anything . . . including math.

Don't think he'll turn pro because he scores more often than other kids. On the other hand, don't think he's destined for a life of geekdom just because he's the worst player. Either way, the odds are he'll be exactly average by the time he's seventeen.

Read the sports section with him. (Reading is reading.)

Keep in mind, if his soccer (or baseball or basketball or any sports) team is more important to you than it is to him, something is wrong. With you.

Three things to
remember if he brings
home a skateboard:
Don't laugh at him.
Don't criticize him.
Don't get on it.

Teach him how to lose
without losing it.
And how to win
without acting like he's
never won before.

Do not tolerate
poor sportsmanship
from him. If you do,
the habit will stay
with him for the rest
of his life.

Tell him
"no pass, no play."
Even if it means he
misses the regional
soccer playoff.

Teach him that just
because he isn't the
best at something,
doesn't mean he can't
enjoy it.

Accept the fact that he may not be a quarterback. He may be a tuba player. And a fine one at that.

Boys &
Spirituality

Remember, your primary duty as a father is to develop your son's spiritual well-being.

Teach him the
difference between
being lonely and
being alone.

Teach him that
success in the face
of adversity is the
greatest success of all.

Teach him that self-esteem can only be achieved by achieving.

Talk to him about God,
about Jesus,
about Moses, about
spiritual leaders often.
Start when he's young
and he won't be shy
talking about them as
a teenager.

Remember, if you can't talk to your son about God, then you've never really talked to him.

Take him to Sunday school or Hebrew school or a religious school regularly. He'll say he doesn't like it. But one day you'll notice you have an outstanding teenager who still insists he doesn't like religious school.

Pray together
as a family, then
teach him to pray
on his own.

When he's confronted
with a serious problem,
encourage him to ask
God for help in
solving it.

Teach him that God answers every prayer. Sometimes with a no.

Teach him God can be trusted.

Teach him to pray
for his enemies.

Teach him to believe that as he gives to the world, so the world will give back to him.

Teach him to give anonymously.

Teach him to treat each day as holy.

Teach him that he can spend an hour complaining about his problems to friends, who can't do a thing about them, or an hour talking to God. Who can.

Teach him that
self-pity is a waste
of time.

Be prepared for him to come home one day a complete agnostic.

Teach him that forgiving someone isn't a weakness, but the height of selfishness—because it makes you feel so much better.

Boys & Money

Give your son an allowance based on his age and the chores he performs. Realize he'll always want more.

Teach him how
to negotiate for
a raise.

Buy him a wallet. Then tell him that whether it's empty or full is up to him.

Teach him nothing is free.

Never be afraid to say, "We can't afford it."

Teach him that if
he wants something
badly enough, that is a
reason to go to work.

If he needs it,
loan him money.
Make him pay
you back.

Teach him to save.
Help him open a
savings account.

Teach him to wait
for sales.

A young boy loses things. A teen who loses things and is made to do without them learns not to lose things.

Teach him that people who value expensive brands too much have lost their sense of values.

Teach him that if you can't buy the best, buy the best value.

When he's twelve, help him buy a small amount of stock with his own money. Think of the rewards he'll reap if he keeps that up for fifty years.

Teach him to pay
his bills promptly.

Teach him how to read a financial page. If you don't know how, learn with him.

Insist he get a job
by age fifteen.
The fact that he doesn't
like it is the last reason
not to make him do it.

o

Show him how to write a check and balance a checkbook. He'll say he knows how, but he really doesn't.

Teach him not to make a bet that he can't settle.

Give him a credit
card and teach him
to use it only
in emergencies.

Teach him to stay on a budget. If he's not a math genius, there are plenty of free, secure online tools to help him do this.

Teach him to never pay list price for an automobile.

Boys & Girls

Let your son know
you're as confused
about women as he is.

Be sure to meet his girlfriends.

Remind him that it doesn't matter if she doesn't have a curfew. He does.

Treat his girlfriends
with respect.
Make sure he does.

Don't embarrass him
when it comes to girls,
although often just
your being alive will be
embarrassing enough.
Still, when he goes to
parties, have no qualms
about calling to see if the
parents will be home.

When you drive him on dates, make sure he gets out of the car to get his girlfriend. You'd be amazed how many boys still think they can just honk and she'll come running.

Think before you react to the notes you find on his desk, the text messages on his phone, or the emails in his computer. It could be something—or nothing at all.

Talk to him frankly about sex. And your expectations of him.

Hug and kiss his
mother often in
front of him.
He'll act disgusted,
but ignore him.

Never criticize his
mother in front of him.
Never, never, never.

Teach him to compliment his mother's cooking. Even when it's liver and onions.

Realize you
can't mend his
broken heart.
You can feed it,
however.

${E}$ncourage him to
ask out that blonde.

Older Boys

Teach him to set goals. Start small. For many teenage boys, just setting the alarm clock is a goal.

Don't let him play Madden NFL for four hours and believe he's been exercising.

Teach him to wash
and fold his laundry.

Remind him that
school isn't a place
for self-expression.
It's a place for learning.

Show him your high school yearbook so that both of you will know how goofy you once looked.

Drive him and his
friends to the movies.
It's a way of learning
who his friends are.

Teach him he has to earn people's respect. Starting with yours.

Talk to him
about his dreams.
And about yours.

Let him fail.
He'll never grow
up otherwise.

Teach him that he can learn as much from failure as he can from success.

Teach him that there's
a direct correlation
between studying and
good grades.

Teach him that most
everything is okay
in moderation.
Including moderation.

Listen to him when he talks—all evening, if that's what he wants.

Remember,
he's watching
how you treat
your family.

Give him
responsibility.
It separates boys
from men.

Don't defend the stupid things he does. If you do, he'll learn he can get away with stupidity. Hold him accountable.

Teach him respect
for books.

Teach him how to
barbecue a steak.
This is a rite of passage.

Make him laugh. Trade jokes.

Hug him before bedtime every night. Even when he's eighteen.

Tell him often
that you love him.

Make sure he spends time around his aunts and uncles, cousins, and grandparents. He may not like all of them, but he'll develop a love for family.

Teach him to
channel his anger.

Teach him that
the only way to
conquer fear is to
confront it.

Remind him often
that he's capable of
changing the world.

Teach him tolerance.

When he's done something wrong, confront him immediately. Don't worry about hurting his feelings. But after you've chewed him out, it's time for you to get over it.

Don't hold a grudge against him.

Teach him the value of wisdom.

Unfailingly, be kind.

Try not to criticize him in front of his friends.

Make sure his friends know that alcohol and drugs are not welcome in your house.

Put his computer
in the family room.
No matter what
he says, he can get his
homework done there.

Don't be alarmed at
the music on his iPod.
Remember, your music
terrified your parents.

Swallow your pride
and ask him to
program the remote.
He'll do it faster
and better, and you
won't wind up in
a bad mood.

Teach him to be on time and to call if he's going to be late. Always.

Teach him the secret to solving even the most complicated problems is to just begin.

Realize a smartphone enables him to access all those websites you won't allow in your house. This is when you have to trust that the morals and values you taught him will kick in.

Stress to him that he has more to learn, whether he's going to college or to a trade school.

At dinner, if he won't tell you about his day, tell him about yours.

Sometimes you will just have to talk to your son about things that will upset him: his behavior, friends using drugs, and so on. This is where a father earns his stripes.

Raise him not to tolerate alcohol or drugs at his parties, and to refuse if offered them at friends' parties. Tell him this does not mean he's a loser. It just means he's smart.

Don't dismiss any dream of his as too big.

Teach him that
jealousy serves
no purpose but to
make him feel bad.

Teach him what's important in life— and it's not a car or the right clothing label or any "thing."

Allow him to wear your clothes, your shoes, your socks as soon as they fit him. When you can no longer find any of your clothes, start borrowing his.

Teach him that
no possession is
worth stealing.

Teach him how to drive. How to drive downtown. How to drive in the rain. How to drive in the snow.

Show him how
to pump gas and
check his tires.
(You would think he
knows, but he doesn't.)

Teach him there are times to stay between the lines. Like on highways.

Teach him to put his car windows up and lock his car at night.

Make his use of the
car conditional,
based on his grades.
He'll become an
Einstein.

Teach him to always wear a seat belt.

Encourage him to give things away.

Teach him that men
do clean up the kitchen
and the house.
Every day.

Until he graduates, set curfews and stick to them. When he's a senior, make a more lenient curfew that's conditional upon his grades.

Encourage him to participate in some kind of community service. This is where giving back begins.

Teach him to buy his mother holiday gifts and Mother's Day cards—and as he gets older, to buy them with his own money.

Encourage him to run for student government. He could wind up the president.

Teach him how
to look someone
in the eye and to
shake hands firmly.

Teach him patience, kindness, and tolerance. If you don't, many years from now you'll wish you had.

Teach him nothing
that he does—
or is going to do—
is ever worth lying to
you about.

Expect excellence.

Teach him to stand up for what's right, even when everyone else thinks he's wrong. Even you.

Let him face the consequences of his actions. They are the best teachers.

Lower the boom on him if he talks back— to you or to his mother. Stop it in grade school and it won't happen in high school.

Teach him to respect his teachers, his elders, the police, even his crazy aunt. Disrespectful kids go nowhere in life.

Monitor his Internet activity and tell him you'll monitor his cell phone, too.

Be prepared to answer difficult questions without editorial comment.

If you've taught him not to get in a car driven by a drunk, he won't.

Lay down strict rules about drinking and driving. Enforce them religiously. If he does wind up in traffic court (and he might), make sure he dresses nicely and respects the judge.

If he's guilty,
do not take his side.
He deserves what he's
about to get. This could
be an opportune time
for him to learn about
apologies and being
cool under pressure.

If he does come in smelling of alcohol, throw the book at him. But that's the only thing.

If he cheats and
gets caught, let him
face appropriate
disciplinary action.
At school and at home.

Teach him that to get along in the adult world, he has to look and act like one.

Teach him to floss.
It will do wonders
for his breath.

Buy him deodorant
and the whole house
will smell better.

Show him how to shave and how to stem the blood from the nicks with wadded-up pieces of tissue. This could save him a fortune in bloodstained shirts.

Don't get freaked
out over his hair.
Just insist he
wash it.

Know the difference between normal teen behavior and questionable teen behavior. Learn to accept and live with your normal teen.

Teach him that trust
is like fine china.
Once it's broken,
it takes a while to put
it back together.

Don't issue an
ultimatum you
can't live with.

Hang a punching bag
in the garage . . .
it absorbs a lot of
sibling rivalry.

Teach him to stand up straight.

Teach him that
there's honor in even
a minimum-wage job.
He'll learn this quickly
if you're not giving him
any money.

Tell him to call his boss if he's going to miss work or be late.

Believe in him.

Remember,
teenage boys like
looking at themselves
in the mirror.
Every now and then
ask him what he sees.

Do push-ups
together.

Show him how
to gargle. If you don't,
your bathroom could
be irreparably harmed.

Realize that you can't be everything to him.

Teach him the joy
of finishing a job.

Teach him that the world will judge him by his actions, not his intentions.

Remind him
to be on time.
Always. The world
doesn't operate on
teenager time.

Don't tolerate
his moodiness,
and you won't have
moods to tolerate.

Teach him that rules—
even dumb rules—
shouldn't be broken.

Make time to hang
out together, just
the two of you.

Teach him how to apologize. Saying "sorry" is not the same as saying "I'm sorry."

Tell him to chew
with his mouth
closed and talk
with it open.

Show him how
to eat with
chopsticks. As well
as a fork and knife.

If you go on a business trip, call him. Tell him you miss him. He may not respond, but it will make his day.

Show him how to change a tire. If you don't know how, get someone to teach both of you.

Teach him that reckless people usually end up doing more damage to others than to themselves.

Teach him that true independence means he pays.

Assure him that having a clean room doesn't make him a nerd. It just means he can find his underwear.

Encourage him to
trust his instincts.
If something
feels unsafe,
it probably is.

Realize that if the two of you do something once, he might think of it as a tradition. (Boys are really weird that way.)

If he's been up late
at night and sleeps
past noon, wake
him up and give
him something
to do.

Teach him that the only constant thing in life is change.

Teach him not to
judge a book by
its cover. Or a girl
by her looks.

Teach him to read
the instructions.

Teach him that
it's possible to
work too hard.

Teach him that the solution to most problems isn't a pill.

Teach him that there's no harm in failure, only in the failure to try.

Show him how
to use a hammer,
a screwdriver,
and a saw.

Teach him not to burn his bridges.

Teach him to treasure his friends.

Teach him to ask
for help.

Show him how to
read a map.

Teach him
to be kind.

Teach him that he's in charge of his own destiny.

Teach him that there is nothing to fear but fear itself.

Teach him how
to iron.

Teach him not
to hold on to
anything too
tightly.

Teach him that appearances do matter.

Teach him to reach for the stars.

Promise you'll always be there for him.

Tell him to never give up.

Teach him to call
his mom.

In the end,

Let him go.